Camel
China, 690–750
Ceramic, 33 inches tall
(B60S95)

The Stone Table Garden by Sun Kehong
China, 1572
Handscroll; ink and colors on paper, 12 x 146 inches
Transfer from the Fine Arts Museums of San Francisco
Gift of Mrs. Edward T. Harrison (B69D52)

Cup with two handles
China, 1662–1722
Porcelain with incised decoration and yellow glaze
1.5 inches tall (B60P2339)

Dragon Fortune by Hung Yi
Taiwan, 2014
Enameled steel, 101 inches tall
Gift of Victor Ou, InSian Gallery (F2016.3)

Ravana, a demon king
Indonesia, 1950–1980
Puppet; wood, cloth, and mixed media
32 inches tall
The Mimi and John Herbert Collection
(F2000.86.31)

Teapot in the shape of a tea crate and stool by Zhou Dingfang
China, 1990–2000
Ceramic, 5.3 inches tall
Gift of Rhoda Mesker (2000.1.a-.b)

Flowering plants and fruits of the four seasons by Watanabe Shiko
Japan, 1725–1755
Six-panel folding screen; ink, colors, and gold on paper, 67 x 145 inches
Gift and Purchase from the Harry G.C. Packard Collection Charitable Trust
in honor of Dr. Shujiro Shimada, _____ Brundage Collection (1991.54.2)

A mandala of the Buddhist deity Shamvara
China, 1800–1900
Colors on cotton, 26 inches tall
Transfer from the Fine Arts Museums of
San Francisco, Gift of Katherine Ball
(B72D5)

Ritual vessel in the shape of a rhinoceros
China, 1100–1050 BCE
Bronze, 9 inches tall
(B60B1+)

Daoist immortal riding a carp by Kosen
Japan, 1900–1925
Netsuke; ivory with detail staining and inlaid horn
1.8 inches tall (B70Y369)

Rectangular pillow with figures in a landscape,
China, 1100–1200
Ceramic with overglaze decoration, 5 inches tall
(B60P2377)

Monkey in the coils of a snake
Japan, 1800–1900
Netsuke; ivory and inlaid wood
1.5 inches tall (B70Y1244)

Spirit guardian
China, 500–535
Painted ceramic
10 inches tall (B64P17)

Wrapping cloth (bojagi) with jewel motif
Korea, 1800–1900
Patchwork silk, 23.3 inches tall
Acquisition made possible by Mrs. Ann
Witter (2002.7)

Theatrical headdress for the magical deer in the
Ramayana dance drama
Thailand, 1950–1960
Papier-maché, glass, and mixed media
19 inches tall
Gift from Doris Duke Charitable Foundation's
Southeast Asian Art Collection (2006.27.10.9)

Go players by Sokoku
Japan, 1800–1870
Netsuke; wood, lacquer, antler,
elephant ivory, and copper alloy
1.2 inches tall (B70Y868)

Pillow
Japan, 1900–1930
Bamboo, rattan, wood, and nails, 7 inches tall
Lloyd Cotsen Japanese Bamboo Basket Collection
(2006.3.385)

Scholar's books and things (chaekgeori) by Yi Eungrok
Korea, 1860–1874
Eight-panel folding screen; ink and colors on paper, 80.3 inches tall
Acquisition made possible by the Koret Foundation, the Connoisseurs'
Council and Korean Art and Culture Committee.
Re-mounting funded by the Society for Asian Art (1998.111)

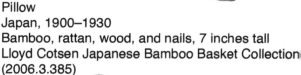

Adventures in Asian Art
An Afternoon at the Museum

by **Sue DiCicco**
with **Deborah Clearwaters** and the **Asian Art Museum**
Chong-Moon Lee Center for Asian Art and Culture

TUTTLE Publishing
Tokyo | Rutland, Vermont | Singapore

Acknowledgments

Timeless thanks to the many artists, from ancient to contemporary, whose incredible artworks are featured in this book. The mastery of skill and the depth of history (and sometimes intrigue!) that each artwork contains was the driving force for us, instilling a wish to introduce young children to them, and to the world of art in general, in an approachable and captivating way. We had the extraordinary good fortune to be guided by the highly informative and supportive museum staff, from museum director Jay Xu to the many curators, educators, and people in other specialties, such as photo services, registration, public relations, graphic design, and editorial. Thanks to you all for your thoughtful input and encouragement over many months. Endless thanks to our friend and Asian Art Museum Trustee Ann Tanenbaum, a tireless and attentive champion for the book. Special thanks and gratitude to Terri Jadick, one of the finest editors we have ever had the pleasure to work with. To Christopher Johns, and everyone at Tuttle Publishing who have been so supportive and enthusiastic, thank you for believing in the vision and allowing us to bring it to reality.

—Sue DiCicco, Author and Illustrator and Deborah Clearwaters, Co-author

A Note to Parents and Teachers

The Asian Art Museum houses over 18,000 artifacts that span millennia and have been gathered from all corners of Asia. This book features 53 of them to give a sampling that traverses regions, time periods, and types of art. We hope you will visit the museum's website with your children and students to discover more of the many treasures that have come from these magnificent parts of the world. You can browse the museum's collection at http://onlinecollection.asianart.org.

The opening and ending pages of this book provide some specific information about the artwork featured here. To find out more about a particular artifact, go to the website cited above and enter the object's accession number (found in parentheses following the size information or credit line) on the "search" line.

Please note that the artworks in this book are not shown to scale. You may be surprised at their actual dimensions. They range from sculptures that can fit in a child's hand to one the size of a car! We hope that imagining these at a size that fosters interaction will be a source of fun for your children and students.

Have a wonderful adventure!

All photographs of artworks are by the Asian Art Museum. Artworks are from the Avery Brundage Collection unless otherwise noted.

An afternoon in Asia,
Just you three and me.
Around the world and back again,
Let's go and look and see!

5

We'll imagine how we might look
In a jeogori jacket tied so neat.
Now let's try the chima and baji,
And special shoes upon our feet.

6

The kids are trying on hanbok, the traditional clothing of Korea. These days hanbok is worn only on special occasions. The bridal robe above has lucky symbols of birds and flowers for a lady to wear on her wedding day. Do you have a lucky symbol?

Ganesha will show the way,
As you sing and dance and play.
This Hindu god brings luck and joy
To every girl and every boy.

His elephant head makes Ganesha one of the most popular Indian Hindu deities. He brings good luck and makes life easier. He also loves sweets! He grabs them with his trunk. His many arms make him very powerful. How many arms can you count?

You'll meet up with the Buddha
And learn the middle way.
The path of peace will set you free
And help you center, day by day.

"Buddha" means "enlightened one." The Buddha lived in India about 2500 years ago. He sat under a Bodhi tree to meditate, and did not move for days. Then, he touched the earth, which shook as if to say "You are enlightened." How many animals can you see surrounding the Buddha? Hint: some are make-believe.

The Indonesian puppet master makes the puppets move and does all the voices to music played on instruments like the ones below, called "gamelan." These puppets tell a famous story called the Ramayana (watch for it later in this book!) Can you guess which puppet is a trouble-making demon?

You'll be a voice of honor
And speak the truth for all.
No matter what you're feeling,
We'll help you stand up tall.

This lion-headed Sky-walker is a Tibetan Buddhist deity. Don't be frightened by her fierce appearance; she helps you rise above your limitations. See the third eye on her forehead? With it, she can see everything. She's dancing. Try standing like her.

You'll dance with the Sky-walker
And clear the path ahead.
You'll carry the fire of wisdom
Through the hair upon your head.

15

The Tibetan mandala is a picture used in meditation. It is an imaginary palace seen from above, and the goal is to get to the center. To get there, you must first pass through a maze of obstacles, The deities hovering around the top are there to cheer you on throughout your journey. How many deities can you count?

When your feet grow weary
And you're much too tired to walk,
A rhino ride will suit you
And give you chance to talk.

This vessel from China might have been used to hold food or a drink.. An inscription inside says it was made by a king to reward an ally for his loyalty. What would you give to somone as a reward?

But, if your load is heavy
And only a camel will do,
Why go with one hump
When life is better with two?

Camel sculptures like this one were placed in tombs to help spirits in the afterlife. Two-humped camels come from Central Asia. Like other types of camel, they can travel for days without water. The two-humped camel can stand all kinds of weather. They helped people carry things very long distances.
Where would you like to go on a camel?

Rhinos and camels are quite nice,
But would you like to fly instead?
I know a winged creature
With horns upon his head.

This bronze make-believe animal from Iran held a horse bit, a metal bar the horse bites on, and which is attached to the reins. The bit passed through the hole on the creature's chest. This creature has a human face. If you were to invent a creature, what would it look like?

Traveling Buddhist monks brought tea from China to Korea and Japan as a medicine to help soothe the tummy and boost energy. Today tea is popular over the world. Some people say tea helps focus the mind and make friends. What drinks do you like to share with friends?

We'll sit awhile when we want to rest,
And share which artworks we like best.
Whichever your favorites may be,
You're my cup of tea.

In East Asia, the dragon symbolizes the power of the ruler. Jars like these were used to hold beautiful handmade flowers. The dragon is a make-believe creature made of many animal parts, like the claws of an eagle.
What other animals make a dragon?

A dragon brings good luck to you,
And keeps you from harm in all you do.
But, through kindness come your true powers.
Your love shines and beauty flowers.

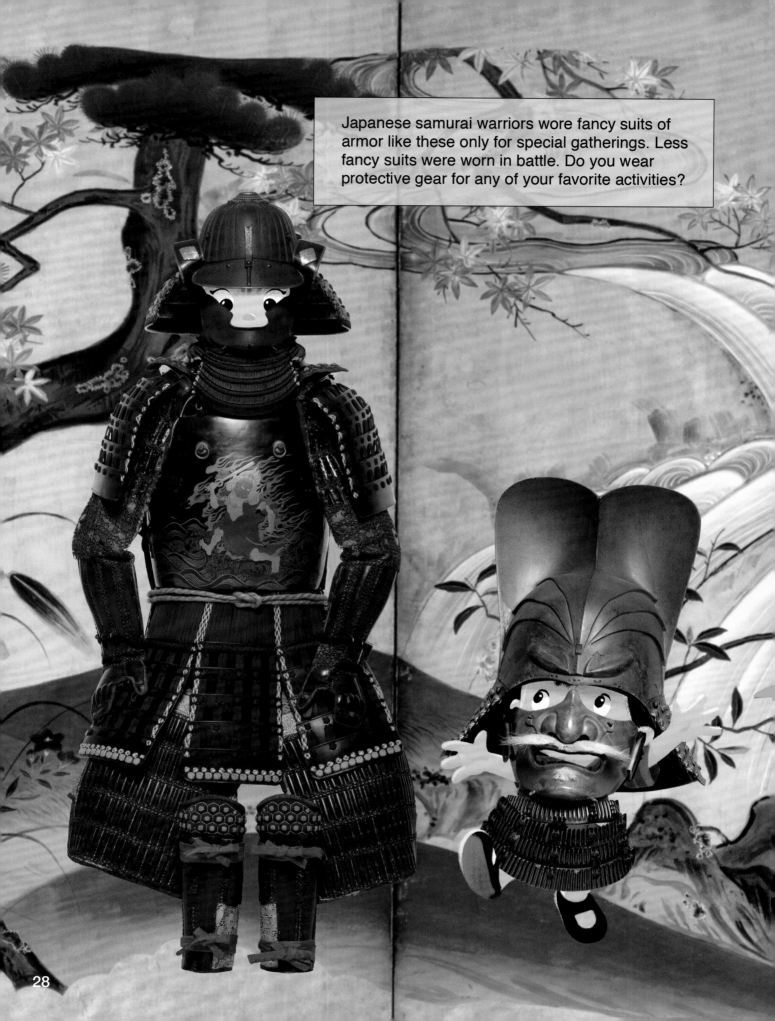

Japanese samurai warriors wore fancy suits of armor like these only for special gatherings. Less fancy suits were worn in battle. Do you wear protective gear for any of your favorite activities?

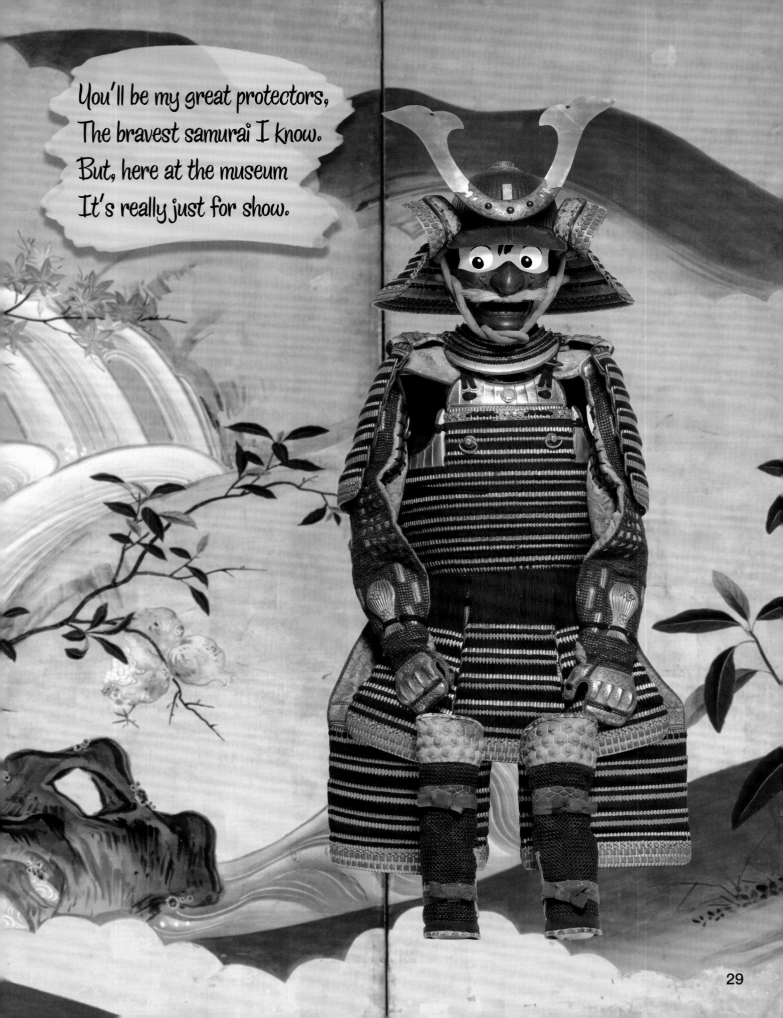

You'll be my great protectors,
The bravest samurai I know.
But, here at the museum
It's really just for show.

Prints like this from Japan showed popular trends. The two young people trying to capture fireflies in their net are wearing the latest summertime fashions of their day. What would you wear to catch fireflies?

This folding screen was painted to look like shelves holding a variety of books and treasures. What items would you put in a painting of your favorite things?

We'll take some time to study
And visit other lands,
If only through their books and art.
The works of hearts and hands.

As soon as we are sleepy
We'll take a little nap.
Your pillows look like pottery.
Mine, a little trap!

These pillows look hard to sleep on, but they are very comfortable once you get used to them, and they keep your hairdo from getting messed up. The bamboo one is for summertime. Can you guess why?

In this ancient tale, called the Ramayana, Princess Sita asks Prince Rama to capture a golden deer. But the deer is a decoy and leads to the princess being captured by the demon Ravana. These crowns from Thailand are worn by dancers performing this famous story. Imagine how heavy they would feel on your head. Do you remember seeing a different kind of art form that tells this story?

Whatever are my wishes,
I know you'll see them through.
I'll trust in you forever.
I know your love is true.

The thing about adventures,
They come both big and small.
And it doesn't make a difference
If you're tiny or you're tall.

These miniature sculptures of animals and people are called "netsuke." Traditional Japanese clothing didn't have any pockets, so people carried small items in a little box that dangled by a cord from their belt. These netsuke were attached to keep the cord from slipping though the belt. What kind of little sculpture would you like to wear?

Teamwork is our way
In our work and play.
Together we are more
Than what we were before.

This Indian painting may be showing circus entertainers. These women playfully imitate a king riding on his camel. What animal shapes can you make with your body?

The Korean bojagi is a patchwork cloth made for wrapping precious objects or to cover serving trays. They were usually made by women for a special person and occasion, like a mother for her daughter's wedding. How do you wrap your treasures?

When our museum tour is done,
We'll buy a special treasure
To give ourselves some pleasure
And remember our day of fun.

Dragon Fortune was made in 2014 out of steel covered with colorful enamel so it can stay outdoors for everyone to see. Taiwanese artist Hung Yi wishes you good luck with this large, colorful beast. What brings you luck?

44

We say our thanks for all we learn
(And can't wait for our return)
To all museums everywhere
That celebrate this world we share.

Around the world and back again,
Wherever we may roam,
You'll remember all we saw and learned
And tell your friends back home.

These strange, spiny-backed figures from China served to guard and protect places and the people in them. How do you protect the people and things you care about?

Published by Tuttle Publishing, an imprint of
Periplus Editions (HK) Ltd.

www.tuttlepublishing.com

Library of Congress Control Number: 2016955286

ISBN: 978-0-8048-4730-8

Distributed by
North America, Latin America & Europe
Tuttle Publishing
364 Innovation Drive
North Clarendon, VT 05759-9436 U.S.A.
Tel: 1 (802) 773-8930
Fax: 1 (802) 773-6993
info@tuttlepublishing.com
www.tuttlepublishing.com

Asia Pacific
Berkeley Books Pte. Ltd.
61 Tai Seng Avenue #02-12
Singapore 534167
Tel: (65) 6280-1330
Fax: (65) 6280-6290
inquiries@periplus.com.sg
www.periplus.com

19 18 17 16
6 5 4 3 2 1

Printed in China   1611 CM

ABOUT TUTTLE:
"Books to Span the East and West"

Our core mission at Tuttle Publishing is to
create books which bring people together one
page at a time. Tuttle was founded in 1832
in the small New England town of Rutland,
Vermont (USA). Our fundamental values
remain as strong today as they were then—
to publish best-in-class books informing the
English-speaking world about the countries
and peoples of Asia. The world has become a
smaller place today and Asia's economic, cul-
tural and political influence has expanded, yet
the need for meaningful dialogue and information about this diverse region has never been
greater. Since 1948, Tuttle has been a leader
in publishing books on the cultures, arts,
cuisines, languages and literatures of Asia.
Our authors and photographers have won
numerous awards and Tuttle has published
thousands of books on subjects ranging from
martial arts to paper crafts. We welcome you
to explore the wealth of information available
on Asia at **www.tuttlepublishing.com**.

All photographs of artworks are by the Asian Art Museum.
Artworks are from the Avery Brundage Collection unless
otherwise noted.

Pillow in the form of a reclining girl
China, 1115–1234
Ceramic, 6 inches tall
(B60P422)

Hunting for fireflies by Suzuki Harunobu
Japan, 1767–1768
Woodblock print; ink and colors on paper, 10.5 inches tall
Gift of the Grabhorn Ukiyo-e Collection (2005.100.29)

Brush holder
Korea, 1800–1900
Porcelain, 5 inches tall
(B60P406)

Suit of armor
Japan, 1615–1868
Lacquered iron plates, leather, textile, and cord, 55 inches tall
Transfer from the Fine Arts Museums of San Francisco, Gift of
Mr. R. P. Schwerin (B74M7.a-.e)

Theatrical headdress for Rama in the Ramayana dance drama
Thailand, 1950–1960
Gilded lacquer, wood, silver, glass, textile, rawhide, and paper, 22.5 inches tall
Gift from Doris Duke Charitable Foundation's Southeast Asian Art Collection
(2006.27.10.10.a-.f)

Birds and flowers
Korea, 1700–1900
Four-panel folding screen
Ink and colors on silk, 84.5 x 81 inches
(B65D43)

Suit of armor
Japan, 1800–1850
Lacquered and gilded iron, silk, bronze, animal hair, and
leather, 48 inches tall
Transfer from the Fine Arts Museums of San Francisco
(B83M12)

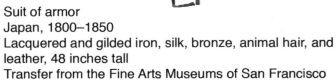

Cup from the Japanese Tea Garden in Golden Gate Park
Japan, 1910–1925
Porcelain, 2 inches tall
Gift of the Hagiwara family (F2010.25.1)

Jar with dragon design
Korea, 1750–1850
Porcelain, 17.5 inches tall
Gift of the Connoisseurs' Council with additional
funding from the Koret Foundation (2008.63)

Wrapping cloth (bojagi) with "tree of life" motif by Han Sang-soo
Korea, 1960–1970
Embroidered silk, 16 inches tall
Gift of Mary C. Stoddard (2001.18)

Rama, hero of the Ramayana
Indonesia, 1800–1900
Puppet; wood, cloth, and mixed media
26 inches tall
The Mimi and John Herbert Collection
(F2000.85.15)

Pillow in the shape of a tiger
China, 1115–1234
Glazed ceramic, 4.5 inches tall
(B60P423)

Theatrical headdress for Sita in the Ramayana dance drama
Thailand, 1950–1960
Gilded lacquer, wood, silver, glass, textile, rawhide, and paper
21 inches tall
Gift from Doris Duke Charitable Foundation's
Southeast Asian Art Collection (2006.27.10.8.a-.d)

Peri riding composite camel
India, 1800
Watercolors on paper, 8.5 inches tall
Gift of Mr. and Mrs. George Hopper Fitch
(1988.51.8)

Teabowl with lotus petals
China, 1127–1279
Glazed ceramic, 3.3 inches tall
(B62P121)

Spirit guardian
China, 500–535
Painted ceramic
12.5 inches tall
(B60P331)

Cat by Masatami
Japan, 1848–1853
Netsuke; elephant ivory, 1.2 inches tall
(B70Y1080)

Wrapping cloth (bojagi)
Korea, 1950–1960
Patchwork silk, 25.3 inches tall
Gift of Dr. Forrest Mortimer (1993.5)